EASTBOURNE

Volume 2

A Second Portrait in Old Picture Postcards

by

John Wilton

S.B. Publications

This book is respectfully dedicated to the memory of

IAN GOW, T.D., M.P.

First published in 1991 by S.B. Publications
Unit 2, The Old Station Yard, Pipe Gate, Market Drayton, Shropshire TF9 4HY

ISBN 1.870708.93.8

Typeset and printed by Delmar Press (Colour Printers), Nantwich, Cheshire

CONTENTS

Front Cover: Tennis at Devonshire Park, p.u. 1914

Abbreviations used in text: p.u. — postally used; c. — circa.

ACKNOWLEDGEMENTS

The author is indebted to the following people without whom this book would not have been possible; for the loan of various postcards (in addition to my own collection):

David Brook — page 94.
The Eastbourne Heritage Centre — pages 30,46.
Eddie Graves — paves 1,2,3,5,9,16,31,65,66,70,71,72.
Chris Hardwick — page 26.
Chris Howden — pages 10,18,19,20,21,24,25,38,40,53,58,61,62,64,69,75,98,105,106,107,109.
Miles Jenner — page 108.
The Reference Section of the Eastbourne Library — page 41.
David Rothwell — pages 42,112.
John Ryder-Smith — page 67.
St. Andrew's School — page 44.
Wendy Slade — page 68.
Chris Taylor — pages 6,50.
John Vincent — pages 76,77,78,79,80,81,82,83,84,85,86,87,88,89,90,91,92,93,95.

Help with additional research: *The Eastbourne Gazette and Herald*; Miles Jenner, Head Brewer, Harvey & Son (Lewes) Ltd.; Major Melvyn Ackroyd, Commanding Officer of the Eastbourne Citadel Corps of the Salvation Army; Neil Collins, City Editor of *The Daily Telegraph*; David Child; John Smith; Eddie Graves of *Memories of Sussex*; Marie Lewis and the staff of the Reference Section of the Eastbourne Library.

Typing: Polly Stone-Lee. Editing and marketing: Steve Benz.

BIBLIOGRAPHY

The Beachy Head Light, R. Armstrong.

Bernard Spilsbury: His Life and Cases, D. Browne & T. Tullett, 1951.

Black Diamonds and White Cliffs, J. Hollands, 1982.

Childhood Memories of Polegate Wind & Water Mills, B. Terry, 1985.

Collect British Postmarks, Dr. J. T. Whitney, 1979.

The Daily Mail, (1912-1913).

Eastbourne Chronicle, (1912).

The Eastbourne Gazette and Herald, (1902-1990).

Eastbourne Local History Society Newsletters — including The Signal Post, Watch Tower and Guns of Beachy Head, Rosemary Milton, Spring 1991.

Eastbourne, a Pictorial History, D. R. Elleray, 1978.

Front Line Eastbourne, T. R. Beckett Ltd. (Gazette and Hearald), 1945.

Grand Hotel, P. Pugh, 1987.

Guide to Eastbourne, R. Armstrong, 1990.

The Guinness Book of Records (1984), Ed. Norris McWhirter.

Old Willingdon, W. J. Vine, 1978.

Moths in the Memory, J. Birdsall, 1990.

A Short History of Eastbourne, L. Stevens 1987.

South Coast Railways — Eastbourne to Hastings, V. Mitchell & R. Smith, 1986.

The Star Inn, Normans Bay, J. Donne, 1963.

The Story of the Eastbourne Lifeboats, J. Morris & D. Hendy, 1988.

The Sunday Express, (1971).

Sussex Murders, D. Briffett, 1990.

Wartime Eastbourne, G. Humphrey, 1989.

There is no Foreword to this book. Ian Gow, the M.P. for Eastbourne from February 1974 until his death, was murdered on Monday 30th July, 1990.

IAN GOW, T.D., M.P.

HOUSE OF COMMONS
WESTMINSTER SW1A 0AA

9th July, 1990

Dear Mr. Wilton,

Thank you very much for having taken the trouble to come to see me at the Eastbourne Office on Saturday morning.

I am so very pleased to have Volume One of your Portrait of Eastbourne in Old Picture Postcards. It really is an enchanting and fascinating book.

I am flattered to have been asked to write a Foreword to Volume Two.

I look forward to hearing from you, when you have selected the items for that Volume.

With renewed thanks.

Yours sincerely,

INTRODUCTION

This second book of Eastbourne, as portrayed in old picture postcards, is in the form of a nostalgic tour which starts in Willingdon. From there we travel through Old Town and Eastbourne town centre until we reach the Grand Parade and pier. Continuing westward through Meads we reach Beachy Head and Birling Gap before turning inland to East Dean, Friston, Jevington and Polegate. From Polegate our tour takes us east to Hankham, Stone Cross, Westham, Pevensey and Pevensey Bay. During the final stage of our journey we make our way back from Pevensey Bay to the Crumbles and from there to Eastbourne pier.

The writing of this book has only been possible thanks to the enourmous amount of help that I have received from my friends, from local postcard collectors and from many members of the public. I am especially indebted to Mr. Oliver Cater who was responsible for the research into the views of Willingdon, Polegate, East Dean and Jevington and to Mr. John Vincent, who not only wrote the notes on Hankham, Stone Cross, Westham, Pevensey and Pevensey Bay, but also supplied the cards from his extensive collection.

New and exciting material continues to arrive on my desk and I can only hope that this book will bring back happy memories and give as much pleasure to its readers as I have had in selecting the postcards, visiting the locations and talking to so many knowledgeable local residents.

John Wilton
Eastbourne
September 1991

Co-author (with John Smith):
Eastbourne, Volume 1; A Portrait in Old Picture Postcards (1990).

THE POST OFICE, WILLINGDON, p.u. 1906

The nearest building is now the village post office but it was originally a bakery and tea room, the change of usage only occurring in 1940. A twitten divides this old building from Pelham Cottage, a small, flint 16th-century building said to be one of the oldest in the village. Pelham Cottage was still thatched at the end of the last century but is now tiled and modernised. In front of these two buildings is the old lime tree planted in 1862 to celebrate the Silver Jubilee of Queen Victoria. The tree had to be removed due to disease but it was replaced by an Acer tree which commemorates the Silver Jubilee of Queen Elizabeth. Partially obscured by the tree is a large ivy-clad house said to have been the home of the village beadle and which contained the village reading room.

CHURCH STREET, WILLINGDON, p.u. 1905

The front doors of the cottages on the left, known as Queen Anne's Terrace, opened directly on to the street from the sitting rooms and these were at first-floor level: the ground floors were below street level and had back doors which opened on to their gardens. Below these, but still on the left was Dick Martin's sweet shop. On entering, customers were almost deafened by an extremely loud cow bell attached to the inside of the stable door as they squeezed themselves into the tiny premises. On the corner of Church Street and Cooper's Hill stands 'The Wheatsheaf', originally two small cottages but later converted into the village beer-house. On the opposite corner stood the Coach House and stables of 'Flint House', now known as 'The Five Gables' which were bought as a parking space and garage to the inn when the car succeeded the horse-drawn carriage. The houses on the right were built in 1904 and replaced two earlier thatched cottages so they would have been newly built at the time of this photograph.

RED LION STREET, WILLINGDON, c.1910

Red Lion Street was part of the main London — Eastbourne road until 1934 and the pub, which achieved literary fame as Farmer Jones' local in George Orwell's 'Animal Farm', is on the left. This is the third 'Red Lion' on the same site: the first was a cottage alehouse, the second a half-timbered house with a mangle room attached where local women could swop gossip and wring out their clothes for a penny a bundle, and the present building, constructed in 1907. In the right foreground, 'The Library' was the village paper shop, tobacconist, confectioner and lending libarary which embodied an earlier bakery. Beyond are Venner's Stores and the Spring Bakery, the latter established in 1873 and expanded by the Venner family to become one of the largest bakeries in the area; baking many thousands of loaves each week and 16,000 hot-cross buns at Easter.

ST. MICHAEL AND ALL ANGELS, OCKLYNGE, c. 1910

St. Michael's Church stands in Ocklynge Road at its junction with Mill Road. The church, with its 102ft-high square tower, was built in 1911. Behind the church is Ocklynge cemetery, formerly known as Ocklynge Piece and consecrated in 1857, which extends as far north as Eldon Road. In the cemetery grounds stand the Episcopal and Dissenters Chapels designed by the architect Benjamin Ferrey who also designed Christ Church in Seaside.

OCKLYNGE ROAD, c.1912

Looking south down Ocklynge road from its junction with Crown Street, J. A. Stribling, fishmonger and poulterer, is on the extreme left. In the centre is John Duke, boot factor, and at the end of the road is the Lamb Inn. (See also Eastbourne, Volume 1, pages 106-107).

THE SEASIDE GIRL, c.1910

There are at least three different cards featuring the Seaside Girl or the Village Belle. The card on the right of page 6 is from a photograph taken on the corner of Ocklynge Road and the High Street, Old Town. St. Mary's Churchyard is in the background. The card has not been postally used but on the back is written: "Very rich lady from Eastbourne who was jilted, and she never went out in her finery but always went out as this photo". This could perhaps explain the article in the *Eastbourne Gazette — Rich Woman in Rags.*

RICH WOMAN IN RAGS

Eastbourne Eccentric again before the Magistrate

Seldom has a more eccentric person figured in a police court than *Miss Clara Wilkinson,* an aged woman of independent means, who yesterday appeared before Eastbourne magistrates for indecent conduct. This was the fourth time she had been summoned for similar offences. She appeared in court dressed in rags, her skirt and blouse being loosely held together with string. A portion of a man's shirt draped on one side. Miss Wilkinson spoke with a refined accent, and stoutly denied any offence. Police constable Martin said he saw her in the midst of a crowd of people. She was dressed in a dirty brown dress, which exposed her legs and part of her body. The defendant, whose method of dressing is well known in Eastbourne, is said to have a large income and wealthy connections. She has paid £9 in fines on account of her dress, which is always ragged. The Chairman yesterday told her that the Clerk would communicate with her cousin in Brighton and her solicitor in Norfolk, with a view to their looking after her. If these inquiries did not end satisfactorily the magistrate would, he was afraid, deprive her of her liberty, though they would be sorry to do so. The case was therefore adjourned for a week.

THE DUKE AND DUCHESS OF YORK'S VISIT TO ST. MARY'S PARISH CHURCH, 1936

The Duke and Duchess of York, together with their daughters Princess Elizabeth and Princess Margaret, are seen leaving St. Mary's Church Old Town after morning service on Sunday, 8th March, 1936. The Duke and Duchess had arrived at Compton Place on Wednesday, 4th March, their daughters joining them one day later, to begin a quiet seaside holiday, the chief purpose of which was to enable the Duchess to recuperate after a recent illness. Just nine months later, after the abdication of Edward VIII, the Duke and Duchess of York became King and Queen of England.

CHURCH STREET, OLD TOWN, p.u. 1905

Looking up Church Street, Old Town before the road was widened. Borough Lane is off to the left. On the corner was Fear's Stores. A. I. Fear, an ironmonger, advertised that he was also a gas fitter and plumber. Next came Cox and Harris, newsagents, where postcards, perhaps even this one, were on sale. Further up the road were Dendy the saddler and O. H. E. Dendy pianoforte tuner. St. Mary's Parish Church is on the right of the picture.

VICTORIA DRIVE, c.1915

Looking down Victoria Drive towards Willingdon and the Downs at the cross roads with Upwick Road on the left and Okehurst Road leading off to the right. The decorative brick pattern above the ground-floor windows of numbers 22 and 20 can still be seen, but that of number 18, on the extreme right, has been covered with weatherboard. The sewer vent clearly visible in the centre left of the picture is still in place today.

LONGLAND ROAD, c.1935

Longland Road runs parallel to Victoria Drive and leads towards the Downs. The photograph, which was taken from the junction of Longland Road and Upwick Road, shows the houses with even numbers. Number 10 is on the extreme right. Very little has changed except for the number of cars now parked in the area.

VIEW OF EASTBOURNE FROM THE DOWNS, p.u. 1907

The view from Uplands Road over the Old Chalk Pit to Upwick and the Borough Sanitorium for Infectious Diseases. The Old Chalk Pit is now Ridgelands, off Uplands Road.

SUMMERDOWN MILITARY CONVALESCENT CAMP, p.u. 1915

Situated in the area now occupied by Compton Drive, Old Camp Road and Pashley Road, the Summerdown Convalescent Camp in 1915 housed up to 3,500 troops. Gardening seems to have been popular and much that did not move was painted white. (See also Volume 1, pages 66-67).

INTERIOR OF A HUT IN SUMMERDOWN CAMP, p.u. 1915

Local photographers, including W. Brooke of Sussex Gardens, Weston of Terminus Road and Crompton's of 32-34 High Street, Old Town were kept busy during the period 1915-1920 taking views of the camp and also more personal photographs of the men in their huts. During the war the camp was visited by King George V and Queen Mary. (See also Volume 1, pages 66-67).

THE DINING ROOM, SUMMERDOWN CAMP, c.1915

The dining room at the convalescent camp was more functional than luxurious. The postcard was published by W. H. Smith in their "Kingsway" series.

THE AVENUE, p.u. 1913

Looking north-east down the Avenue, Upperton Gardens are on the left and Commercial Road leads off to the right. Horse-drawn cabs wait for custom. The iron railings around Upperton Gardens were removed during the war when much of the area was badly damaged. Numbers 20 to 27 The Avenue have been replaced by a large block of retirement flats.

ST. ANNE'S CHURCH, UPPERTON GARDENS, c.1910

The design of St. Anne's Church was probably the combined work of the local architect H. S. Spurrell and G. C. Haddon of Great Malvern. The church, consecrated in November 1882, was described at the time as 'the Church of the Gilbert Estate . . . in the aristocratic Upperton district'. After surviving several near misses earlier in the war, St. Anne's was destroyed by incendiary bombs on the night of 11th August 1942. The church was finally demolished in 1955.

EASTBOURNE RAILWAY STATION, p.u. 1906

In 1846 a link up was made by the London Brighton and South Coast Railway to Polegate. The Eastbourne branch line then followed and was opened on the 14th May, 1849. On that day a special train ran from Brighton to Eastbourne. The train arrived shortly after midday to the strains of a brass band and a celebratory lunch was then served in a large booth erected in the grounds of Orchard Farm. Later this was the site of the Technical Institute and Free Library until its destruction by bombing in February 1943, and is now the site of the Eastbourne Central Library in Old Orchard Road.

(See also Volume 1, pages 84, 86 and 87).

INTERIOR OF EASTBOURNE RAILWAY STATION, p.u. 1914

A rare interior view of Eastbourne Station. This, the fourth station erected on the site, was built in 1886 by F. D. Bannister, engineer to the London, Brighton and South Coast Railway. Platforms 3 and 4 (main line branches) are on the left. In the centre is the registration office for continental baggage and excess luggage and on the right are platforms 1 and 2. On the extreme right, Maple and Co., Auctioneers & Estate Agents, advertise that they are at 116 Terminus Road and opposite the station.

EASTBOURNE RAILWAY STATION, p.u. 1908

During the War, numerous bombs were dropped in the immediate vicinity of the railway station. On 14th March 1943 a fighter-bomber dropped the bomb which tore up track between platforms 2 and 3. It was here that London evacuee children arrived at Eastbourne between 1st and 3rd September 1939, and from here in July 1940, Eastbourne school children were evacuated to Hertfordshire and Bedfordshire to remove them from the invasion threat.

THE SNAILWAY TRAIN, p.u. 1916

When this card was postally used, the journey from Victoria or London Bridge to Eastbourne (65¾ miles) took from a little under an hour and a half to two hours. The fast trains between London and Eastbourne ran via Croydon, Lewes and Polegate. The ordinary fares were: single, 1st class, 10s. (50p); 3rd class, 4s. 8d. (23p). Returns were available for six months, 1st class, 17s. (85p); 3rd class, 9s 4d (47p).

THE GYMNASIUM, YORK ROAD, c.1924

The gymnasium was located in York Road, near the Town Hall. An advertisement in the *Eastbourne Chronicle* on Saturday, 5th January, 1924 informed readers that classes would be held during the Christmas holidays. These would include a Family Class for girls and boys on Mondays, Thursdays and Saturdays, at 10 o'clock. A Boxing Class for boys on Tuesday and Friday at 10 o'clock, a Fencing Class for ladies on Tuesday and Friday at 11 o'clock. Private lessons for Swedish physical exercises, boxing, fencing etc. Medical gymnastics and Swedish remedial exercises could also be arranged. For further particulars readers were asked to apply to a Mr. Moss.

TERMINUS ROAD, c.1906

Looking down Terminus Road towards the railway station. In the central background, on the left, is the Brighton Arms, the licensee at the time was a Mr. J. Davies; to the right of the pub is the Lewes Old Bank, which was destroyed by a 500kg bomb in March 1943. Next to the bank are The Barclays Bank Chambers and then further right again, John Pring & Co., furnishers, decorators and upholsterers.

BOBBY'S, TERMINUS ROAD, c.1950

Looking down Terminus Road from its junction with Lismore Road. Bobby's now Debenhams, is on the left. Marks & Spencer's is in the centre of the picture and Pevensey Road leads off to the right. The history of the "Bobby" shops commenced in 1900, when Bobby's of Margate, which Mr. F. J. Bobby purchased in 1887, was established by him as a limited company. Subsequently stores were acquired at Leamington Spa, Folkstone, Eastbourne, Torquay, Cliftonville, Bournemouth, Southport and Exeter. (See also Volume 1, page 94).

THE TEA ROOMS, BOBBY'S, TERMINUS ROAD, c.1950

In 1950 Bobby's celebrated their Golden Jubilee by providing their customers with a special Jubilee Tea. This consisted of: toasted tea cake, Indian or China tea, brown or white bread and butter, apricot jam, Jubilee Cake and a Neapolitan ice. All this was provided for the sum of 2s. 6d. (12½p).

THE DEVONSHIRE PARK THEATRE, p.u.1910

The Devonshire Park Theatre was designed by Henry Currey and opened in 1884. The entrance is flanked by two handsome Italianate towers which house the fireproof emergency staircases. In 1903, much of the interior was remodelled by Frank Matcham. (See also Volume 1, page 74).

THE INDIAN PAVILION, DEVONSHIRE PARK, p.u.1910

The Indian Pavilion was designed by T. E. Collcutt in 1892, and first erected for the Royal Naval Exhibition at Chelsea that year. Later it was re-assembled in the Park and used for refreshments and dressing rooms. The Pavilion was demolished in 1963 to make way for the Congress Theatre.

TENNIS AT DEVONSHIRE PARK, p.u.1907

The Devonshire Park is still one of the leading tennis centres in Britain, hosting several important tennis tournaments. Behind the players are the Devonshire Park Theatre, the Water Tower of the Swimming Baths, and on the right the Floral Hall.

THE SUSSEX HOTEL, CORNFIELD TERRACE, c.1920

The card is inscribed "Dad's outing, Eastbourne", and the charabancs are seen parked outside the Sussex Hotel in Cornfield Terrace. The shop, No. 24 on the left, is M. L. Giles and Co., ladies' outfitter. In 1914 the Sussex offered bedrooms: single 3/6; double from 6/-; breakfast from 2/-; luncheon from 2/6; tea from 1/-; dinner 3/6. Boarding terms: 10/6 per day; 63/- per week.

AFTER THE GREAT BLIZZARD, 1908

Looking east towards the Queen's Hotel and Pier, the carpet gardens are hidden under a blanket of snow. Eastbourne, often referred to as the 'suntrap of the south', has nevertheless had some memorable winters, including that of 1908-9, with great blizzards in December and snowstorms in March. (See also Volume 1, page 31).

THE GRAND PARADE, c.1906

Standing with our backs to the pier and looking across the Grand Parade towards the hotels, now mostly in a poor state of repair. This cannot be said of the Queen's, in the right background, which is still one of the premier hotels in the town. Notice the Eastbourne Corporation open-topped 'bus on its way to Meads. (See also Volume 1, page 39).

THE SAND ARTIST, p.u. 1905

Mr. Albert Edward (Ted) Child, the sandscratcher featured on this card, was a member of an Eastbourne family who also held the concession for the fruit stalls along the promenade. At the turn of the century the favourite pitch for the artist to work was just west of the pier. The pictures usually depicted the main cathedrals, castles or warships. Often the pictures were accompanied with a short poem or proverb — on completion of the picture the artist would place his cap to the fore of the "sand cathedral" and the spectators would show their appreciation by throwing pennies from the pier. The pitch was prepared as the tide went out by digging and draining the area. The tools that the scratcher used were pieces of old box-wood to mark out the pictures and then wires from the same box would be twisted into a fan-shaped rake so that the area could be texturised.

THE GRAND PARADE BANDSTAND, p.u.1935

Large crowds congregated at the newly opened Grand Parade Bandstand which provided seating for 3,000 people and replaced the earlier "bird cage" bandstand. The Grand Parade Bandstand, also known as the Central Bandstand, was opened on August Bank Holiday, 5th August 1935, by Lord Leconfield, Lord Lieutenant of Sussex. The cost of the development was £28,000.
(See also Volume 1, pages 23 and 25).

THE EASTBOURNE LIFEBOAT, p.u. 1904

The *James Stevens No. 6* pictured outside the William Terriss Memorial Lifeboat House — now the Eastbourne Lifeboat Museum. In 1898, the R.N.L.I. decided to provide Eastbourne with a new lifeboat and boathouse. A fund to pay for the boathouse was raised by the *Daily Telegraph*, to commemorate the well-known actor William Terriss who was assassinated outside the stage-door of the Adelphi Theatre in London the previous year. On Saturday, 16th July, 1898, on a site near the Wish Tower, Her Grace, The Duchess of Devonshire, laid the foundation stone of the new boathouse. The new lifeboat arrived at Eastbourne in October 1899. It was one of 20 lifeboats that were built out of the magnificent legacy of £50,000 from Mr. James Stevens of Birmingham. The James Stevens No. 6 was launched 43 times during the period 1899-1924 and 34 lives were saved. (See also Volume 1, page 21).

THE EASTBOURNE LIFEBOAT, p.u. 1910

The card shows the *Olive* being hauled out of the William Terriss Memorial Boathouse for an exercise launch. In 1902 it was decided to open a second lifeboat station at Eastbourne and so a corrugated iron boathouse was built at the Fishing Station, east of the pier. This is still in use today. A 36ft. x 9ft. Liverpool Class, non-self-righting lifeboat was built at a cost of £839, this being defrayed from a legacy of the late Misses Wingate of Edinburgh, with the boat being named the *Olive*. During the summer season the *Olive* would remain at the Fishing Station boathouse with the *James Stevens No. 6* at the Wish Tower. For the rest of the year, the positions were reversed.

SUNDAY PROMENADE ON THE WESTERN LAWNS, c.1906

Standing on the Western Lawns, facing the north-east towards Martello tower No. 73. the Wish Tower. The photograph was taken before 1910 as there is not, as yet, a statue of the 8th Duke of Devonshire in the centre foreground. The hotels on the left include the Lansdowne and the Wish Tower. (See also Volume 1, page 12).

MIXED BATHING AT EASTBOURNE, c. 1914

A local guide book at the time stated: The beach is of shingle, gradually sloping, flat sand as the tide recedes. The bathing-machines are well appointed. Mixed bathing is popular. Bathing without machines is prohibited on any part of the shore between 200 yards east of the Redoubt and the Wish Tower on the west. Strong swimmers can take a header from the pier head any morning between 6am and 9am. Fee 4d.; season tickets, 6s.

CHASELEY, SOUTH CLIFF, c.1912

Chaseley on South Cliff is now a home for severely disabled people, mostly paraplegic ex-servicemen. It is a non-profit making registered home supported by the D.H.S.S. The house consists of three floors and a basement and there is a beautiful terraced garden on the south side from which there are magnificent views over the sea and looking towards the Downs. Chaseley was originally a grand private house owned at one time by Lady Michaelis. Her son was blinded in the early stages of the war and she wanted to give the house and £50,000 to the nation as a home for blind ex-servicemen. However, owing to the proximity of St. Dunstan's near Brighton, discussions were held with the then Minister of Pensions and as a result Chaseley was opened as an auxiliary hospital for paraplegic ex-servicemen in November 1946.

SILVERDALE ROAD, p.u.1911

Little has changed in this road except that the horses have been replaced by cars and many of the elms by cherry trees. Compton Street is off to the right and the Grand Hotel is situated behind the camera.

SOUTH CLIFF AVENUE, p.u. 1908

It was in this quiet residential avenue that at about 7.15 on the evening of Wednesday, 9th October, 1912 a burglar was seen lurking in the shadows. The man was lying silently on the flat porch over the door of No. 6, the house of Countess Sztaray, the daughter of an Hungarian nobleman and an English mother. The police were called and within minutes, 44-year-old Inspector Arthur Walls arrived. He called to the man to come down. The only reply was a shot. The Inspector staggered back having been shot through the heart.

THE FUNERAL PROCESSION OF POLICE INSPECTOR WALLS, 1912

On 16th October, 1912, Inspector Arthur Walls was buried in Ocklynge Cemetery. The card shows the funeral procession passing the Royal Hotel in Terminus Road. The *Eastbourne Chronicle* reported: "All classes of inhabitants as well as the chief representative bodies, combined in a remarkable demonstration of sorrow at the loss of a martyr to public duty and an honourable, fearless and genial officer . . . The Eastbourne Borough Force, represented by Chief Constable Major Teale and about fifty officers and men preceded the funeral car, which was drawn by a team of four horses." A few days later, a John Williams was arrested and charged with Inspector Walls's murder. He was tried at Lewes Assize Court, found guilty and hanged on 28th January 1914. But now, as then, there are those who are not convinced of John Williams's guilt.

ST. PETER'S CHURCH, MEADS ROAD, c.1907

St. Peter's Church was designed by Henry Currey and stood at the corner of Meads and Granville Roads. Although a listed building, it was declared redundant and later demolished in 1971. The area is now occupied by Redman King House — sheltered housing for the elderly.

EASTBOURNE COLLEGE, c.1872

The card is a reproduction from an early photograph of Eastbourne College and the surrounding area taken in 1872 from the newly completed tower of St. Saviour's Church in South Street. The building on the skyline in the centre of the picture is Cliffe House, also known as "Earp's Folly", which at that time was the home of William Earp. It was this William Earp, who, in 1875 made the original planning application for the building of the Grand Hotel. The hotel was completed in 1877 and then managed by Earp. In the foreground, what is now School House, stands by the intersection of Blackwater Road and College Road. There is not, as yet, any sign of the College Chapel, which was built on the left of School House and consecrated in 1874. (See also Volume 1, page 72).

ST. ANDREW'S SCHOOL, p.u. 1914

St. Andrew's School, founded in 1877, is one of the few private schools still to be found in Eastbourne. But this was not always so. In 1932 a report stated: "There are 380 private schools, and they practically rule the town. During the summer vacation they allow different organisations to use the schools for boarding houses". (See also Volume 1, page 56).

ALDRO SCHOOL, p.u. 1909

At this time the boys of Aldro preparatory school used the playing fields by All Saints Hospital for their games of cricket. Aldro moved to Shackleford near Godalming at the start of the second world war and has remained at its Surrey home ever since. The fields are now used by St. Bede's School, which can be seen on the left. In the centre of the picture is St. Luke's Children's Hospital with All Saints' Convalescent Home and its chapel on the right. The photographer is standing with his back to Chesterfield Road and looking westwards towards the Downs. (See also Volume 1, pages 2, 6 and 7).

MEADS STREET, c.1910

Looking south down Meads Street, the view is similar today. On the extreme left, was C. O'Hara Ltd., the Meads butcher, now occupied by Meads Carpet Centre, note the delivery bicycle propped against the wall. Numbers 19, 21, 23 and 25 are also shown with Derwent Road leading off to the left. On the far side of this road are numbers 27 and 29, built on the site of the Old Ship Inn. The Downs are visible in the background with a 'bus travelling down Meads Street on its way to the Railway Station. Nine shops with flats above, even numbers 54 to 36 still stand on the right. The shop on the extreme right, on the corner of Matlock Road, is now Thresher's wine merchants. (See also Volume 1, pages 58-59).

MEADS STREET, p.u. 31st March, 1904

The 'bus on the left of the picture was used by the World's Oldest Municipal Omnibus Service inaugurated on 12th April 1903 between Eastbourne Railway Station and Meads. The card was sent to 1 Matlock Road, which joins Meads Street from the left about 100 yards further down, with the recipient Miss E. J. M. Breach, invited to "Look out and catch this motor". The shops, featured in the centre of the picture, are still there today, as is the Ship Inn, but the houses on the right have been replaced with a block of flats — Meads Gate.

KING GEORGE V AND QUEEN MARY AT HOLYWELL, 1935

The visit of King George V and Queen Mary to Eastbourne, during February and March 1935, is well documented in the *Eastbourne Gazette.* On Saturday 16th March, the King and Queen motored to the Wish Tower and walked to Holywell along the lower parade. Unfortunately a mist, which drifted off the sea, tended to reduce the pleasure of their Majesties' walk, and they did not remain at their chalet. King George and Queen Mary used chalet number two at Holywell until their return to London on Tuesday, 26th March. (See also Volume 1, page 5).

WESTERN BEACH AND CLIFF, p.u. 1910

The photographer is standing near to the western end of the lower promenade and looking south west towards Beachy Head. The steps on the right lead up to the then derelict Gore Chalk Pit. In 1922 this pit was converted into the Holywell Italian Gardens. (See also Volume 1, pages 4 and 5).

EASTBOURNE. Coast and Beach.

HOLYWELL HAMLET, c.1900

The card shows Holywell Hamlet and the pumping station erected by the Eastbourne Waterworks Company. The coal for the steam-powered pumping station, was brought to the beach at Holywell by colliers. Men would unload the coal in buckets and then reload the ship with chalk. (See also Volume 1, pages 3-4).

STEWART THORPE'S MEMORIES OF MEADS, 1880-90

When I was a boy the hollow now called Holywell was not so called — it had no name. It was just an old unused chalk pit. I believe chalk used to be taken away in boats. Sailing boats used to run aground here and men loaded them with blue boulders from the beach. We believed they were taken to Lancashire where the flints were used in the making of glass. The real Holywell is the next hollow. Springs of clear water ran out of the chalk face. In the hollow were a colony of fisher-folk with their cottages and boat sheds. When I was 10 or so they were made to move out and it is now (1895) occupied by the Eastbourne Waterworks Co. They installed a pumping station to make use of the constant supply of water that fed the springs.

As far as I can remember the fishermen were chiefly interested in crabs and lobsters. Some shrimping and prawning was done. Scallops could often be bought for 3d. a dozen. Some men gathered limpets and winkles from the rocks. In season sprats were sold by the 100. The small trader piled his sprats on a tray and took them round on a hand cart but when they were plentiful they were brought round on a horse drawn dray. Under the cliffs opposite the landing place there was a gap in the line of rocks. Possibly man made but it allowed only 2/3ft. on each side of a fishing boat entering the "lagoon".

The fisherman's objection to fires on the beach may have been that the light would have been considered as a signal to French smuggling boats that all was clear. There were times when the small boats from Holywell went out well beyond their usual limits and came back loaded with more than fish. Occasionally we youngsters helped to carry bundles, bales and ankers (small casks) to a pit in front of the boat houses. This pit was some 8 to 10 feet deep and 18 feet long and 8 feet wide. It had a covering of planks and on these was a large boat — keel up. It all looked very innocent. The coastguard had a good idea of what might be going on but by this time they had moved up to Beachy Head, so as one of them said to me years later, "Why should we bother to walk all the way down there. Possibly no smuggling had been done and if it had the stuff would have been shifted away and well hidden long before we got there".

SURREY BRIGADE CAMP, p.u. 1912

Members of E. Company march along Foyle Way on their way to Whitebread Hole. Behind them, on the left, is Holywell Mount, which during the 1950s the home of Jack and Gertrude Hullett, patients of Dr. Bodkin Adams. Dr. Adams received money from Mr. Hullett's estate and later from that of Mrs. Hullett. The Police suspected wrong doing, but after Dr. Adams was found not guilty of the murder of Mrs. Edith Morrell, another of his rich patients, they decided not to bring further murder charges against him. Holywell Mount is now part of St. Bede's School campus. The main school buildings can be seen on the right. (See also Volume 1, page 2).

CHURCH PARADE, SURREY BRIGADE CAMP, July 1912

This was the scene during a Church Parade for The Surrey Brigade camped in Whitbread Hole. Eastbourne Pier is just visible on the extreme right of the picture.

MEMORIAL SEAT AT BEACHY HEAD, c.1930

The seat and plaques erected to commemorate the purchase by the Eastbourne Corporation of the Downs, from Beachy Head to Folkington, for the preservation of the amenities of Eastbourne. A tablet, upon which the above is inscribed, was unveiled by His Royal Highness The Duke of York, K.G., on the 29th October 1929. The seat and plaques were damaged and removed during the war, but were resited near to their original location. This fact is commemorated by a plaque unveiled on 21st November 1979 by His Grace The Duke of Devonshire P.C., M.C.

EAST SUSSEX HOUNDS MEET AT BEACHY HEAD, 1924

This rare card was produced from a photograph taken by a local photographer "RH". It shows the Meet of the East Sussex Hounds at Beachy Head in March 1924. The East Sussex were founded in 1853 and amalgamated with the Romney Marsh in 1966. (See also Volume 1, pages 76 and 114).

THE WATCH TOWER, BEACHY HEAD, c.1914

A watch tower was constructed at Beachy Head and local coastguards undertook signalling on behalf of Lloyd's. The watch tower was leased by the corporation of Lloyd's from His Grace the Duke of Devonshire in December 1882. It was rebuilt by Lloyd's in 1896, purchased by Lloyd's in 1897, and formed a part of Lloyd's signal station at Beachy Head until 1904, when signalling work for Lloyd's was transferred to the adjoining naval station where since then it has been conducted for Lloyd's (July 1932).

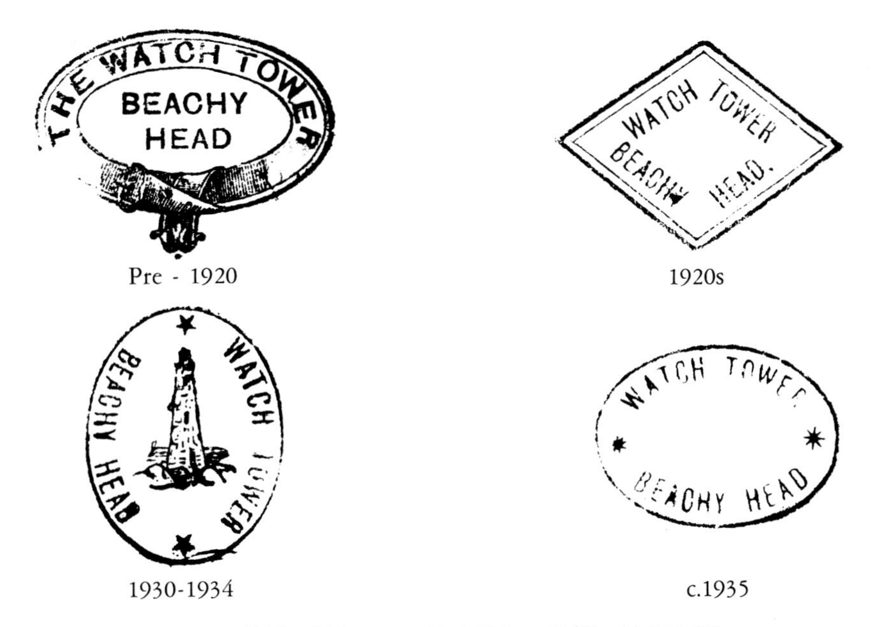

Pre - 1920

1920s

1930-1934

c.1935

WATCH TOWER, BEACHY HEAD CACHETS

During a period, roughly coinciding with the interwar years, when the watch tower was no longer needed for its original purpose it was transformed in to a kiosk selling postcards, stamps and films. The cards were stamped with a watch tower, Beachy Head cachet for visitors. In later years the watch tower fell into disrepair and was tidied up by the removal of the upper structure above the windowsills. One side of the base was left open giving access to a telescope, through which panoramic views could be seen.

BIRLING GAP HOTEL, p.u. 1905

The Birling Gap Hotel stands on land owned by the National Trust. During the last one hundred years, the sea has eroded the cliffs at the gap at an average rate of 2.8m a year and parts of the hotel are now only about 25m from the edge. The Hotel has recently been refurbished and a large restaurant added on the landward side. When the above photograph of the Hotel was taken there was a 9-hole golf course at Birling Gap.

BIRLING GAP, c.1920 (left) p.u. 1953 (right)

The two cards give some indications as to the rate of erosion of the soft chalk cliffs. The white line gives the approximate position of the cliff edge in 1991.

EAST DEAN CHURCH, c.1904

Perhaps the most famous vicar of East Dean and Friston was the Reverend Jonathan Darby who took over the parish in 1706. A Sussex man whose father had been vicar of Ashurst, Jonathan Darby cut himself a cave some twenty feet above the high water level in the cliff below the present Belle Tout lighthouse, about one mile west of Beachy Head. On stormy nights he would climb the steps he had carved out to 'Darby's Hole' and keep watch to warn off, or help ships driven onto, the treacherous reefs along this coastline. The vicar died of pneumonia in 1728 and his gravestone in this churchyard states simply that "he was a friend of sailors". His history can be found in more detail in the porch of the church and visitors should also look for the sundial above the church door and the lychgate across which the groom must lift his bride after their wedding service. (See also Volume 1, page 119).

THE GILBERT INSTITUTE, EAST DEAN, p.u. 1907

The Gilbert Institute was a gift to the village of East Dean from the Davies-Gilbert family of Birling Manor. Built in 1884 it has served as a library, a doctor's surgery and a Sunday School as well as a village hall, although the older inhabitants of the village still refer to it as 'The Reading Room'. It is now only one of four community meeting places in the village and its main present function is as a base for the mobile library. The striking flint building has a cottage on either wing with the hall spanning the central area.

THE NAVAL VOLUNTEERS AT EAST DEAN, c.1914

The Naval Volunteers gathering on the village green outside the Tiger Inn, following their recruitment at the start of the first world war. The ever popular village green, now with its memorial and maypole, has changed little since this photograph, although the rough flint track which led from the road to the Tiger and the adjoining cottages is no longer used as a parking place for visiting vehicles. The cottage next to the public house is known as 'The Cub'. It is possible that the Tiger Inn itself is misnamed, as the heraldic device of the Bardolf's of Birling, medieval owners of the manor, was a leopard and the name of 'The Tiger' may have arisen as a result of poorly informed identification.

THE OLD FORGE, EAST DEAN

On the lower slopes of Friston Hill was the forge and cottage of the village blacksmith. The last blacksmith, Luther Hill, was appointed here and lived in the cottage from the time of his retirement after the last war until his death at the age of 94 in 1964. The cottages at the bottom of the hill were occupied by the farmworkers of Gore Farm which, along with other farms in the village, were still using carthorses during the second world war, although tractors had invaded the rural scene in the mid-nineteen twenties. Behind the workers' cottages is the current village hall; then two loose boxes which served as the village mortuary when occasion demanded.

EAST DEAN

The road to East Dean from Eastbourne was still unmade in 1920 and there was no gas or electricity in the village. When the road was constructed during the early 1920s local flints were used as a foundation. There are stories of local carters taking the same load of flints past the check-in point where their chitty was signed, only to turn off over the Downs before they reached the construction gang and present the same flints after a suitable lapse of time. The Gore Farm, seen on the right at the bottom of the hill, provided most of the cheese, butter and milk for the village. In the early days of motorised transport some milk was transported to Hoadley's dairy in Eastbourne in a 'Maxwell' lorry, while a horse and cart served the village.

GORE FARM, p.u. 1909

Gore Farm — the word 'gore' is Saxon for the end of a triangular piece of land — was mentioned in the Domesday Book. The house stood on the site of two present-day chalet houses, next to the garage at the foot of the hill, but was demolished by Atlantic Richmond in 1970 when the garage and the house changed hands. The present garage grew from the initial installation of a petrol pump in 1924. The farmer at that time, E. O. Hobden, grew tired of requests to tow Model T Fords to the top of the hill because their gravity-fed fuel system was inhibited by the slope, and invested in the pump to ensure they has sufficient petrol to make the journey unaided. At the time of this picture there were no more than a dozen houses where the East Dean and Friston estates now stand, all of which were connected with the farm. The horses in the foreground were probably those of Mr. Russell, who farmed here for many years before Mr. Hobden, and who owned or was tenant to over 1000 acres of land.

FRISTON CHURCH AND WINDMILL, p.u. 1904

Friston was a larger and more important village than East Dean until the time of the Black Death when it was virtually wiped out. The church is still there for all to see but not the windmill which stood on the northern side of the present coast road, between the B2105 to Jevington and the present entrance to the housing development. All the land to the right of the windmill — dramatically free of housing on this card — was part of East Dean's Gore Farm and only the sale of the farm after the war led to the considerable building programme of the 1940s and 1950s. The sails of the mill blew down in a gale c.1925, but a family called Wettleson lived in Mill Cottage for many years and finally, in the 1940s the lower part of the building provided a home for the much-loved village post lady, Madelaine Lillie and her mother.

When the building was demolished in the 1950s an estate agent's office occupied the site.

JEVINGTON, p.u. 1908

Travelling along the B2105 from Friston towards Polegate, the first view of the lower end of Jevington village has changed little since this photograph was taken. The photographer was standing at the end of Eastbourne Lane and the house on the right, beyond the figure, is now the 'Hungry Monk' Restaurant, formerly a butcher's shop and 'The Monk's Rest' tea rooms and guest house. Opposite the 'Hungry Monk' are some cottages belonging to Jevington Stud and the entrance to Church Lane which leads past St. Andrew's Church and is part of the South Down's Way. Beyond the restaurant on the right is 'Hawthorn's General Stores' which has been replaced by a modern bungalow and stabling.

THE EIGHT BELLS, JEVINGTON

Nobody really knows why Jevington's popular public house was called 'The Eight Bells' or what, if any, seafaring connections formerly existed: perhaps it was only that the 'last watch' of the day providing hard working locals with the opportunity to take their ease. In the days of licensed houses, The Bells was only one of five such establishments in the village, a license being granted to one Joseph Seymour sometime between 1800-1810. Seymour sold the premises to a Seaford brewer called John Gorring for £600 and immediately leased it again for seven years. The wall in the foreground of the picture was removed in 1960 to make room for a new car park as the previous parking space — to the left of the water cart on the road — held only six cars. In 1969 the pub was extended and a new entrance created below the 'Teas' sign in the picture — saving those who had over imbibed from staggering straight out on to the road.

THE OLD POST OFFICE, JEVINGTON, p.u. 1908

The Old Post Office in Jevington was situated in one of three cottages built at the Polegate end of the village but which is now a private dwelling although the name has remained. The Post Office was transferred to a site incorporating the village hall on the bank below Devonshire Cottages before the last war and remained there until the early 1960s when its closure left the village without this facility. One of the other cottages in the terrace pictured above held a drinking license for a short time in the mid-19th century.

POLEGATE WINDMILL

Polegate Windmill was built in 1817 by one Joseph Seymour who became an important landowner in this part of Sussex. The mill is of the tower type being substantially of brick construction unlike the other two types of mill; the post and smock, which were of wood. In 1967, exactly 150 years after its construction, it was reopened having been restored by the Eastbourne and District Preservation Society, whose Trust now owns it.

THE HORSE AND GROOM, POLEGATE, p.u. 1907

At the turn of the century Polegate High Street ran outside the front door of the Horse and Groom public house, seen here in the left foreground. The tall tree which dominates the centre marked the entrance of Southdown Hall Estate — now Old Drive. Southdown Hall was the residence of the Diplock family from 1873-1936 and was situated near where Southdown Court flats now stand. Further down the street is the Jubilee Tree planted by Miss Sarah Matilda Diplock in 1887 to celebrate Queen Victoria's Jubilee year. The tree partially obscures the cottages which still remain as numbers 1 and 3, St. John's Road.

ST. JOHN'S TERRACE, POLEGATE, c.1902

In the background are the level crossing and rather imposing railway buildings which once stood on this now empty site. The actual station had been moved some four hundred yards towards Eastbourne by the time this picture was taken, but it has since been returned to almost its original position — minus the more impressive architecture of former days. The left-hand shop of the pair nearest the camera was the Post Office between 1900 and 1915 and by 1922 a third shop had been added.

POLEGATE RACES, 1907

A very rare card produced from a photograph taken at Polegate Races on 24th April 1907.

THE SCHOOL, STATION ROAD, POLEGATE, p.u. 1914

The first maintained Polegate School was an infant school which opened in 1850 in the building which is now a new church for the 7th Day Adventists in Hailsham Road. The school in the photograph was constructed in 1894 in the area known as Swine's Hill, the road being known as Station Road after the station had been moved, and became the infant and junior school for the village until 1990 when the last group of children moved to newer premises in Oakleaf Drive.

POLEGATE STATION, p.u. 1919

In 1907 there were an impressive network of crossings where today only two lines suffice for the rail traffic. The railway did play a part in the growth of Polegate, even if that growth was not immediately obvious in the mid-19th century. In 1846 rail passengers for Hailsham or Eastbourne had to alight and continue their journey on foot or by coach. In 1849 spur lines were added to Eastbourne and Hailsham and a branch line to Hastings in 1871. In 1881 the station was moved to its Polegate Inn site, but later resited nearer the level crossing and High Street.

THE DOG HOUSE, HANKHAM ROAD, HANKHAM, c.1908

This L-shaped 17th-century timber-framed building was originally three cottages, but was converted into a single dwelling some years ago. Above the front door there is a gryphon crest of the Duke family of Laughton Lodge; an interesting Grade II listed building. The name "Dog House" is connected to its earlier inhabitants, the Customs and Excise officers. This is the former home of the late Member of Parliament for Eastbourne, Mr. Ian Gow.

LUSTEDS, GLYNLEIGH ROAD, HANKHAM, c.1910

During the 1930s this attractive thatched cottage was destroyed by fire and replaced by another house. A farm closeby still retains the name of "Lusteds".

HANKHAM TEA GARDENS, p.u. 1910

Chapman's Charabanc from Eastbourne arriving at the Tea Gardens. Visits were a very popular Edwardian pastime. The building has an 18th-century front to a probably older timer frame. It is now a private dwelling known as "The Cottage".

HANKHAM STREET, HANKHAM, p.u. 1912

A pleasant view of Hankham Street which has now changed considerably. The blacksmith's and wheelwright's shop on the right has been replaced by a garage and the cottages further along the lane have been demolished to make way for modern houses.

BLACK NEST, STONE CROSS, c.1910

Black Nest is on the road from Stone Cross to Hailsham at the junction with the road to Hankham. If you were to stand in the same position today, very little has changed over the years.

BLACK NEST, STONE CROSS, c.1910

Westley Gearing and George Fuller outside their wheelwright's shop. The weatherboard building was demolished in 1990 to make way for the Pevensey and Westham bypass flyover of the Stone Cross to Hailsham road.

THE RED LION PUBLIC HOUSE, STONE CROSS, p.u. 1907

The single-storey extension to the right was originally a shop but now forms part of the bar. This building has hardly changed during the last 80 years apart from a meeting hall built between the wars.

FLORAL RETREAT, TEA GARDENS, HIGH STREET, WESTHAM, c.1910

Mr. and Mrs. Casson and their young daughter are photographed outside their shop and very popular tea gardens. To the left of the house there was a large greenhouse with a grape vine. The grapes from this vine were sold in the shop.

HIGH STREET, WESTHAM, p.u. 1913

The fine timer-framed house on the left is possibly the best example of a 15th-century house in the village. Here again, the High Street has hardly changed over the years.

PEVENSEY AND WESTHAM RAILWAY STATION, p.u. 1912

On 27th June, 1846 Pevensey and Westham saw its first steam locomotive when the railway line between Lewes and St. Leonards started a regular service. It was not until 1935 that the line was electrified. Note the milk churns and gas lamps on the platforms.

PEVENSEY CASTLE HOTEL, WESTHAM, c.1906

A most imposing mid-Victorian public house totally out of character and scale with the buildings in the High Street. The coach house to the left was demolished several years ago to make way for car parking.

PEVENSEY FIRE BRIGADE, c.1911

Pevensey Fire Brigade was formed in 1911. This horse-drawn hand pump was donated to the village by Mr. Charles Allen, the owner of the Mint House and a generous local benefactor. It was previously owned by the Eastbourne Fire Brigade and had become surplus to their needs, so the pump was advertised for sale at £175. The price Mr. Allen paid was never disclosed. The original fire station was in a flint building at the rear of The Smugglers public house in the High Street.

THE OLD MINT HOUSE, PEVENSEY, c.1912

Perhaps one of the best known antique shops in the country. Originally three cottages converted into three shops and purchased early this century by Mr. Charles Allen who made the whole building into "The Old Mint House". On this site the original Pevensey Mint is said to have stood. Note the motor-cycle with a wicker sidecar in the left foreground.

THE "HARRIERS" AT PEVENSEY CASTLE, p.u. 1908

Regular meetings of the Marsh Harriers took place at the Royal Oak and Castle Hotel. As can be seen from the rare postcard, they attracted many followers.

PEVENSEY PAGEANT, 1908

A rather stylised view to advertise the Pevensey Pageant. Additional detail has been added to an original photograph taken from the tower of St. Mary's Church, Westham. The Pageant was well advertised throughout the South-East with special train services from London (Victoria). There was a cast of over 2,000 performers and a covered auditorium for 4,500 spectators paying between 3/6d. and 21/- for seats; the event attracting thousands of visitors to the village. Due to the lavish expenditure of the organisers, the Pevensey Pageant was run at a great financial loss.

PEVENSEY PAGEANT, 20th JULY, 1908

The procession lead by the Bishop of Chichester for the official opening ceremony in Pevensey Castle. Perhaps the most important event for Pevensey this century, the Pageant lasted six days depicting in music and prose the history of Pevensey from the "Coming of the Romans in B.C. 54" to the "Smuggling Days of 1746".

RICHMOND TERRACE, PEVENSEY BAY, p.u. 1908

This view has hardly changed over the years. Several of the cottages in the terrace have been converted into shops at street level.

MARTELLO TOWERS, PEVENSEY BAY, c.1910

Martello Towers 61, 62, 63, 64, 65 and 66 stretching away in the distance towards Langley Point. They were originally built in 1806 as a coastal defence against possible Napoleonic invasion. The four cottages in the foreground were built in 1906 by Val Prinseps. This view is now impossible due to modern housing estates in the area.

PEVENSEY SLUICE, NORMANS BAY, c.1912

It has not been possible to obtain any information on the little group outside the signal box. Do any readers know the names of the family group?

THE STAR INN, NORMANS BAY, c.1908

The original building dates back to 1402 and became a public house around 1597 when the name was changed from "Sluice House" to "The Star". The Inn has a long connection with smuggling in Sussex. Towards the end of the last century a storm breached the sea wall and flooded the whole of the "Sluice" area. The Star Inn became a "Noah's Ark" for days and the landlord had to retreat upstairs and take his sheep and pigs with him until the flood subsided.

THE CRUMBLES MURDER, LANGNEY, 1924

On Tuesday, 15th April, 1924, Londoner Emily Kaye, who was then three months pregnant, died at the hands of her lover Patrick Mahon. Mahon, a married man, removed her head, legs and arms which he burnt in the two grates of the Officer's House, a former coastguard cottage on the Crumbles; a bleak bank of windswept shingle.

THE CRUMBLES MURDER, LANGNEY, 1924

He then stuffed the dismembered body into a trunk and when the stench became unbearable he cut portions from the torso, boiled them in stewpans in the kitchen and then cut them into smaller pieces. These he wrapped in bits of Emily's clothing and placed them inside a Gladstone bag, and then back in London caught a late night local train and threw them out of the window. But a suspicious wife and a cloakroom ticket led Patrick Mahon to the gallows. He was arrested by police at Waterloo Station where he had gone to collect the Gladstone bag from the left-luggage office. In it was bloodstained women's underwear, a ten inch long carving knife, some disinfectant powder and a canvas tennis-racket case with the initials E.B.K. marked on it. Mahone was tried at Lewes Assizes in July and was found guilty of murder. He was executed at 9 a.m. on Wednesday, 3rd September, 1924.

Even before the verdict of guilty came in, the bungalow on the Crumbles was being turned into a macabre shrine. There were guided tours at a shilling a head and postcards were available of the bungalow because it became so notorious. According to a Mrs. Laycock who's family lived in the murder bungalow from 1936 to 1940 — "There was no running water. The toilet consisted of an outside hut together with a bucket, portions of newspapers and sand. Honeysuckle and roses covered the bungalow walls. As the house was known by holidaymakers as the murder bungalow, they loved to have photographs taken outside. Mum would have two holidaymakers at weekends for bed and breakfast. This was to the joy of the visitors who could say they had actually slept in the Mahon murder bungalow."

The bungalow on the Crumbles has now been demolished.

PATRICK MAHON RETURNS TO MURDER BUNGALOW, 1924

When on Tuesday, 6th May, Mahon was charged with murder at Hailsham Court his solicitor, Mr. Charles Mayo of Eastbourne asked permission for his client to attend the inquest. This was opened the next day in the sitting room of the Crumbles bungalow. Mahon was led in under tight police escort. About a thousand sightseers surrounded the building and he could hear their boos and jeers as he went in and out, but saw nothing, covering his head with a heavy overcoat.

OPEN TOP TRAMCAR, WARTLING ROAD, c.1960

Mr. Claude Lane founded Modern Electric Tramways Ltd. and operated six miniature tramcars carrying passengers, chiefly holiday-makers, on a 2ft. gauge track. The line opened in Eastbourne in July 1954 and a further extension in 1958 brought the route to nearly one mile. Unfortunately animosity arose between the Corporation and the company over financial matters, the latter deciding that a new operating site was desirable. As a result of this, all equipment was moved to Seaton in Devon, where operations commenced on 27th August 1970.

THE REDOUBT MODEL VILLAGE, c.1963

In 1957 a model village was opened in the central area of the Redoubt. The Manager of the Redoubt Model Village was Mr. Benjamin White, who had designed the buildings and also did most of the construction work himself. Towards the end of the 1970s, after the death of Mr. White, the village was phased out and the Redoubt's parade ground area was paved over.

A STREET — EASTBOURNE MODEL VILLAGE, c.1963

Mr. White's sense of humour is clearly demonstrated in this card, where we find Ted Scragg, family butcher, next to D'ethwatch, Fiddlepenny and Watnoe-Bidd — estate agents, valuers, auctioneers.

ROYAL PARADE AND REDOUBT, p.u. 1906

Looking east down the promenade towards the Redoubt fortress. The Redoubt, formerly known as the Great Redoubt, was the depot for the Martello towers which were erected as defences against Napoleon at the beginning of the nineteenth century. It was completed in 1807 and mounted eleven guns, was surrounded by a moat 35-40 ft. in width and had accommodation for 350 men, with provisions and water for several weeks. From 1853 until 1858 the Redoubt was garrisoned by artillerymen. It was threatened by the sea as the unprotected land on both sides had been eroded, but the construction of long groynes and the extension of the sea wall removed the danger. In 1925 the fortress was purchased by the town and opened to the public.

CHRIST CHURCH, SEASIDE, p.u. 1906

The church is a predominently flint building, designed by Banjamin Ferrey and opened in 1859. Christ Church was patronised by Princess Alice during her stay at Eastbourne in 1878 and the Chancel has a memorial window to her which records the Princess's premature death from diphtheria later that year.

ALL SOUL'S CHURCH, SUSANS ROAD, p.u. 1908

All Souls' Church was designed by the London architect Alfred Strong in Italian Romanesque style. It was built in 1882 with money provided by Lady Victoria Wellesley, a great-niece of the Duke of Wellington. On the left of the photograph can be seen the 83ft-high free-standing campanile.

E. JOLLIFFE & SON, 19 SUSANS ROAD, c.1914

In 1913, according to Gowland's Eastbourne Directory, 19 Susans Road was owned by N. E. Stevens, builders' merchants, but in 1914 ownership passed to E. P. Jolliffe, decorators' supply stores. E. P. Jollife also owned premises at 38, Commercial Road at this time.

THE SALVATION ARMY CITADEL, LANGNEY ROAD, c.1912

The Eastbourne Citadel Corps, founded in 1890, flourished under the command of Captain Jennie Pearson and Lieutenant Fee. But when in 1891, the Corps band started to march through the town on Sundays — an act prohibited by Clause 169 of the Eastbourne Town Improvement Act 1885 — bitter battles resulted, mobs attacked the Citadel, and large crowds jostled and abused the musicians. Many Salvation Army members were arrested and there was a constant stream of Salvationists going to and from Lewes Prison. In September 1892, however, a Repeal Bill passed through Parliament. Marching with music was permitted and gradually the animosity decreased.

QUEEN ALEXANDRA'S COTTAGE HOMES, SEASIDE, p.u. 1907

Queen Alexandra's Cottage Homes, for aged and deserving folk of Eastbourne who were required to pay only a "peppercorn" rent of a penny a week, were opened by the Duchess of Devonshire in 1906. In 1912, by the generosity of the Reverend H. Alston, a wing was added as a memorial to the late King Edward VII. In 1924 the homes were further expanded when a new block and a matron's house was added. The card shows the residents ouside their cottages, the men proudly wearing their campaign medals.

THE LION INN, SEASIDE, c.1940

On Sunday, 10th November, 1940 at 10.10 a.m. the Lion Inn in Lion Lane, Seaside was destroyed in a German bombing raid. Mr. Charles Rich the licensee of the pub was killed and Mrs. Rich was seriously injured. It is reported that several bombers dropped at least twenty-eight bombs. Five fell in the sea, four on marshland behind Astaire Avenue and nineteen made a long line from near the Albion Hotel and directly on the Lion Inn, to Dennis Road (now Dursley Road). Mr. Rich is pictured standing by the front door of his pub.

Mr. SALMET, THE DAILY MAIL AVIATOR, c.1912

During the summer of 1912, Mr. Henri Salmet, the Daily Mail aviator, flew on a promotional tour around the country. According the the *Daily Mail* of 13th June 1912 ". . . with the object of making the English people more familiar with the marvellous progress which flying has made." The paper reported that the Bleriot monoplane, the Gnome motor and the Lavasseur propellor had all come out of the test extraordinarily well. Mr. Salmet held the British record for the high flying (9,000 ft.), the record for speed between London and Paris (3 hours 12 minutes), and the world's record for distance over sea (80 miles).

PASSENGER SEAPLANE AND MARINE PARADE, p.u. 1914

An early seaplane taking off from just east of the pier. In the background is Marine Parade and, from left, the Old Sea Houses, where Charles Darwin stayed for a time in the 1850s while working upon *Origin of the Species*, the Albion Hotel, now empty and in a poor state of repair, and the Albermarle Hotel. (See also Volume 1, page 42).

EASTBOURNE FROM THE PIER, p.u. 1905

An unusual early view of Eastbourne taken from the seaward end of the Pier. The white facade of the Burlington Hotel stands out on the left and the Queen's Hotel is clearly visible on the right of the picture.

WE HAVE LEFT UNDONE . . .

Risqué seaside postcards are nothing new. This one, sent in 1929, was most likely published in large quantities and then overprinted to order with the name of any sea-side town as required.